Through The Bible With Poetry
(A poetic journey through the bible)

By Michael Beatty

All scripture references are from the New International Version (NIV) unless otherwise indicated.

BLOG Site: http://throughthebible.biz
Retail site: http://stores.lulu.com/msbdesign

ISBN 978-0-6151-8530-9

Preface

This book is dedicated to my grandfather, William F. Lay Sr. who was instrumental in helping to form my belief system and moral compass, as well as my mother Shirley who dealt with me before I allowed Christ into my heart.

What I am attempting to do with this volume is to make the younger generation, and anyone else that has a desire, aware of some of the more prominent parts of the bible.

I have accomplished this by picking out certain highlights from each book of the bible, and composing a poem about them. At the end of each poem, I have also included the scripture source for it.

I hope this will provide encouragement for the reader to further search God's infallible word for a source of learning and encouragement.

Since accepting Christ into my heart, I have come to realize that the bible is an important tool for obtaining strength and hope in my life. Until I started writing this book, I was not as familiar with the bible as I should have been. I hope to pass on some of the insight and promise to those that search the pages of this fascinating and insightful guidebook to the Christian faith.

As a bit of information about the format of the poetry in this book, you will find most of the poetry as being tightly rhymed. The only exception to this is the poem that is based on 1st Corinthians Chapter 13. This was my inspiration for the creation of this book and the first poem I wrote in the book.

Please pray the prayer at the end of this book if you have not yet received Jesus Christ as your personal Lord and Savior, and do not know of His strength, grace, and salvation.

In Christ
Michael Beatty

Table Of Contents

NEW TESTAMENT

Old Testament
Laws

involve

killingly

a criufice

New

When God created the world it was a mass,
Of nothing at all but vapors and gas.
Blackness, it seemed, was the only thing around.
There was no sea, nor was there any ground.
God decided that this was not right,
So He shouted out loud, "Let there be light!"
God was pleased with what he had done,
And that was the end of day number one.
The second day came and God made the skies and the seas.
And on the third day, He created the land, grass, and trees.
Day number four was an exciting one.
That's when God formed the moon and the sun.
The fifth day was filled with lots of glee.
That's when God made the animals on land, the birds of the sky,
And the fish in the sea.
Then on the sixth day, God finished His plan.
That's when He made Eve from Adam, the first woman and man.
On the seventh day, God decided to rest.
He was proud of His work, and loved humans the best.

Genesis 1: 1-31
Genesis 2: 1-3

The Commandments

God said to Moses while he was on the hill,
Tell the people that these things are my will:

I am your God. There are none above me,
I am the one to set my people free.
None shall make images and bow unto these,
For my will, this indeed will not please.
Follow these commandments and all will be good.
For I am your heavenly parent, and expect you to do as you should.
No one on earth may use my name in vain.
The meaning of this is really quite plain.
Remember always the Sabbath day,
Because this is the time to rest I say.
Honor your earthly father and mother,
And never ever kill your brother.
Do not cheat upon your spouse,
For this will cause discord in your house.
You must not steal from your fellow man,
Because this disturbs the heavenly plan.
Do not lie in an attempt to save your soul.
Telling the truth is what will make you whole.
Lastly, tell my children not to envy the possessions of others.
If everyone lives under the laws I have set down,
then all can live as brothers.

Exodus 20: 1-20

Blessings Abound

The Lord made a promise to those who obey,
That whatever they do will turn out ok.
He would give them rain for the crops to grow,
And see to it that the fruit bearing would not be slow.
He promised them that wherever their heads they did lay,
He would keep them safe both night and day.
He promised to be with them wherever they would go.
And the rich rewards of His blessings, they would always know.

They had no reason not to believe
Because they knew that God does not deceive.
He brought them out of Egypt and freed them all.
From the bounds of slavery, under which they surely would fall.
Now they could all walk with their heads held high,
Praising God as they looked to the sky.

Leviticus 26: 3-13

Moses Shows His Anger

Now Moses had tired of listening to people gripe and groan,
For forty years he had been on his own,
Watching people shed their tears,
And openly express their anger and fears.

This time it was lack of water they feared,
They were afraid their bodies would be seared,
By the sun's hot rays,
From the heat of the awful wilderness days.

So Moses went to the Lord and asked,
"What should I do, the people are mad, and no
longer want to follow you."
That's alright said the Lord to Moses,
Just take this rod and speak to the stone,
Water will come forth and the people will no
longer moan.

Moses was angered by the people below,
If they needed proof, then proof he would show.
Moses yelled at the people saying, "Must we show you water?"
He struck the rock twice with the rod, and there was abundant
drink for every father, son and daughter.

But Moses was wrong in what he had done,
For the people thought it was him, and not God
who had beaten the drought and sun.
And God had told Moses that for his sin,
He would get to the promised land, but never enter in.

Numbers 20: 7-13

The Song of Moses

Now Moses wanted the people to listen, and listen they did:
Hear my voice, and let my teaching fall like the rain. The Lord is our God
and we shall do whatever He may bid.
You People are bad,
And because of this I am sad.
God gave your father's the land that was good.
He found Jacob wandering in the wilderness,
and did what any loving father would.
He nurtured and cared for him when he was down,
Built him up and gave him the run of the town.
But the people of Israel had too much of a good thing.
So they made other gods and to them they would sing.
The Lord was angered and spoke of His plan,
To send pestilence and serpents to every woman and man..
For a full generation there was nothing but trouble and war,
And every manner of living was a tremendous chore.
Then finally when none of the original did remain,
The Lord started to relieve some of the pain.

Moses warned them to obey the Lord,
Or feel the power of His sword.
They were so close to the promised land,
And everyone around thought it was just grand.
Moses said to remember God,
And they would always tread on fertile sod.

Deuteronomy Chapter 32

Jericho Falls

Jericho was sealed up tighter then a drum,
Because no one came to it, and none left from.
It was a mighty fortress, impenetrable by man,
But the fall of Jericho was in the Lord's plan.
Now the Lord told Joshua to listen well,
To the instructions He was about to tell.
Take your men and march once around the city wall.
This you shall do for six days in all.
Give seven horns to seven priests who will carry
the ark of the covenant ahead.
Tell them not to fear, for they have nothing to dread.
On day number seven, march seven times around the wall,
Blow the trumpets, have the people shout,
and it will fall.
Joshua followed the instructions to the letter,
And because he did, the outcome was better.

We too, must take heed,
And follow the bible when we are in need.

Joshua 6: 1-27

Samson And Delilah

Samson was strong, this was indeed true.
But the secret of his strength was known to only a few.
Delilah was the one that Samson sought
But it seems that Delilah could be easily bought.
The Philistine rulers promised her all kinds of gold,
If the secret of Samson's strength to them she told.
So one night she asked, what made him weak.
He gave an answer but the truth he did not speak.
For when Delilah did as he said,
He snapped the ropes as though they were thread.
Delilah asked again, upset at Samson for the lie he
told.
Samson lied again, wanting to grow old.
So Delilah prodded him and begged for him to be fair,
So Samson succumbed and told her his strength was
in his hair.
So while he slept, all snug and sound,
Delilah with a razor came sneaking around.
Samson was caught now, this much was true.
He was thrown in prison, had his eyes gouged out,
But still he had the faith of few.
He knew he would die but had one last request.
He asked the Lord to make his strength the best.
The Lord had done as Samson had asked,
And Samson placed his hands between the pillars,
And the temple had crashed.

Judges 16: 4-3

A Devoted Woman

The story of Ruth is among the tragic ones,
Of Elimelech, Naomi, and their two sons.
Now Elimelech died in Moab from
the stress of the trip from Judah.
His sons soon married two Moabite girls,
whose names were Ruth and Orpah.
Not too soon after, the boys had died,
And the childless women cried and cried.
The famine in Judah had ended and things
began to settle down,
So Naomi decided to go back
to her old hometown.
She told the girls to stay right where they were,
Orpah did but Ruth decided to go with her.
She gave up all for her father in law's wife,
She'd no longer lead the easy life.
When they returned to Judah Ruth joined
the other poor women
Picking up grain to live on left over by the men.
Boaz saw Ruth and inquired,
Why are you here, what has transpired?
Ruth explained the situation,
And asked him to marry her based on tradition.
Boaz explained there was a kinsman closer then he,
But if that one could not fulfill the obligation,
then her husband he would be.
Sure enough the other man could not come through.
Boaz and Ruth became one, though they were two.
Naomi's estate was spared,
Because Ruth had shown that she really cared.
God smiled down on her for this selfless thing,
For her son was the grandfather of David the king.

Ruth

David and Goliath

Now, Goliath was a Philistine,
Who really liked fights and drinking wine.
He offered a plan to the Israelites,
Who really did not like to get into fights.
"Send a man to fight me". He began to say,
"And if indeed he beats me, the Philistines will
be your slaves this day.
But if I beat him, which I can do without much
fuss,
Then you and your people will be slaves to us."
This went on for forty days,
Till David, youngest son of Jesse, appeared from the haze.
He was on an errand to deliver food,
When he heard Goliath being rude.
The Israelites scattered as they had done before,
But David was strong, for the armor of God was what he wore.
David's brother Eliab scorned him severely,
And even Saul the leader, didn't believe him really.
But David persisted and Saul gave in,
He gave him the Lord's blessing and hoped he would win.
He dressed David in armor and sent him out that day,
But David could not use it, for it hindered him in every way.
David took his staff and five smooth stones,
Faced down Goliath and listened to his tones.
Goliath taunted him and came closer still.
David put a stone in his sling, slung it at Goliath
and hit him in the forehead.
Moments later the giant was dead,
Then you and your people

1 Samuel 17: 1-51

15

David's Song of Praise

The Lord had delivered David from all that was bad,
And David spoke to Him in a song.
He sang of the savior who gave him happiness
when he was sad,
The one that gave him strength to go on,
when the road was long.

He sang of how when he cried to God,
He heard his every plea,
And all his enemies were vanquished
From both the land and sea.

David sang of the rewards from God,
For righteousness based on degree.
David's land was full of rich and fertile sod.
He kept himself clean and pure. A humble servant
of the lord, he would always be.

2 Samuel Chapter 22

Solomon Asks for Wisdom

Solomon, David's son, was a good man
who loved the Lord.
He followed the law and became strong
in the word.
God knew this and appeared to Solomon in
a dream one night
And said ask what you want and it will
be granted because you
have done right.
Solomon asked for understanding, to judge
the people right,
For this was one thing he always wanted
to keep in sight.
The Lord was pleased with the request
And felt Solomon's wish was the best,
Because he had not asked for power or health,
A long life or excessive wealth.

So the Lord granted Solomon's desire,
And took it even one step higher.
Not only did he receive an understanding heart,
But power and riches right from the start.

1 Kings 3: 1-14

Leprosy Healed

Naaman was a leader in Syria's very strong force,
A mighty man of valor, but leprosy was taking it's course.
A captive girl from Israel spoke of a prophet that could heal,
So Naaman went to the sovereign to make an appeal.
The king agreed and sent Naaman on his way,
With a letter to the king of Israel asking
him to heal Naaman on that very day.
The king of Israel was quite upset,
But Elisha the prophet told him not to fret.
Send Naaman to me and once he has seen,
His flesh shall be restored and his body made clean.
Naaman appeared at Elisha's house,
And a messenger came out, just as quiet as a mouse.
Dip in the river Jordan seven times was what the messenger said.
Naaman was quite upset and his face turned a bright shade of red.
He felt Elisha should have called on the Lord
And healed him through the power of the word.
He felt there were better rivers to wash within.
He turned and left, angry and full of sin.
His servants convinced him to do as he was told,
So he dipped seven times in the Jordan getting dirt and cold.
But when he got out his flesh was restored and his body made clean.
Yes he even went back to Elisha to show him the marvelous scene.

2 Kings 5: 1-14

David's Fame

The Philistines heard of David's rule over Israel,
And remembered how their champion, Goliath fell.
So they set out to search for him, to try and make him fall.
David heard of this, and upon the Lord he began to call.
"Shall I go against them, in this your holy land,
Oh Lord will you deliver them into my hand?"
The Lord said yes, go against them and you will win,
For they have intentions that are driven by sin.
David had done as he was told,
And won yet another battle against his enemies of old.

The Philistines again tried to make a raid,
But David knew the foundation for victory had already been laid.
So he asked the Lord what he should do,
And the Lord did more then just give him a clue.
Circle around the troops you see,
And listen for marching among the mulberry tree.
Then go out and strike on the camp,
And once and for all, you will put out their lamp.

Because of David's obedience to God above,
He had his enemies fears, and his followers' love.

1 Chronicles 14: 8-17

Jehoshaphat Threatened

Jehoshaphat, the king of Judah, was a troubled man.
A group of jealous armies had a destruction plan.
Some of his faithful servants came to warn him of the coming day.
Jehoshaphat was scared and asked the Lord to show him the way.
The king ordered a fast, and gathered the people of his land.
He fell on his knees, prayed a heartfelt prayer, and asked
God for deliverance through His mighty hand.
The Lord spoke to the king, and told him not to fear the mobs angry prod,
For the battle did not belong to Jehoshaphat but to God.
In the morning go down against your enemy,
Do not lift a sword in battle, but sing praises unto me.
So Jehoshaphat did as he was told,
The enemy was defeated and the king collected all the gold.

2 Chronicles 20: 1-26

Ezra Confesses

The world before Jesus was a terrible place,
Because holy people would marry those of the pagan race.
When Ezra heard of this horrible sin,
He was full of turmoil and rage within.
He tore his robe and plucked the hair from his head.
He fell to his knees and spoke to the Lord with fear and dread.
Oh my God, was how he started,
From your ways, my people have departed.
You told us the people of this land were unclean,
we knew it from the start.
But our minds and flesh succumbed, to the desires of the heart.
Lord you warned us but we heard you not,
And fell headlong into Satan's plot.
Cleanse us Lord from this stain within.
Guide us so our redemption might begin.
In order for the situation to be resolved,
These pagan marriages had to be dissolved.
So Ezra called a meeting of all the people in the land
And dissolved all the pagan marriages through the power of God,
and by His hand.

Ezra 9: 1-15

Jerusalem Rebuilt

Jerusalem's walls were in ruin for over 140 years,
When Nehemiah came to the king, eyes filled with tears.
He wanted to rebuild his father's city,
Since the people of Jerusalem were filled with fear and self pity.
The king granted Nehemiah's request,
Sent him back to his homeland, and wished him the best.
Nehemiah's task was not an easy one.
His enemies wanted to keep him on the run.
They said that they would go and tell the king,
That Nehemiah's plan was just an ego thing.
Without the Lord's guidance Nehemiah just could not win.
Surely he would succumb to the peoples' sin.
So Nehemiah did what any God fearing man would do,
He asked the Lord to give him a clue.
Half the men were given mortar and bricks to build the wall,
And half had weapons drawn to answer the battle's call.
Without much incident the wall was completed,
But Nehemiah's enemies were still not defeated.
He had to show his people that he was chosen by God,
To tread very carefully on Jerusalem's fertile sod.
Three things had yet to be done,
For the battle he had fought to really be won.
Regular worship was the first thing in line.
A commitment to family was number two to make things shine.
And finally a commitment to obey God's law was added to the list.

With these three things, a social decay, both them and we are able to resist.

Nehemiah Chapter 2

Esther As Queen

Ahasuerus in the third year of his power,
Decided to have a feast in his own honor,
and named the day and the hour.
The feast was beautiful and lasted seven days.
The king called for Vashti the queen, to gaze upon her beauty and give
her praise.
But Vashti refused to go before the king,
And was thrown out of the kingdom because of this thing.
So the king sent out a decree for a new queen and wife,
And it just so happened that Esther, a Jew, was ready for a brand new life.
But she did not let her heritage be known,
For very surely, into the fire, she would have been thrown.
Now Mordecai had raised Esther, and was an attendant in the court.
Esther followed his every instruction, being very careful to never fall short.
In time she was given the position of queen,
And the king threw another ball,
the likes of which the kingdom had never seen.
Her cousin who raised her saved the king from a coup,
So his name went into a book, and he could not be killed even though
he was a Jew.
Haman an Agagite was promoted to a very high place,
And all were to bow when they saw his face.
But Mordecai would not bow to this mortal man,
Because he knew it was not part of God's very glorious plan.
Haman was enraged, but had to take heed,
He could not harm Mordecai because of his great deed.
So he developed a plan to kill all of the other Jews instead.
Surely Mordecai would bow if all of his kin were dead.
Esther found out of this evil deed,
And devised a plan so her people could be freed.
She planned two meals, both grand and fine,
And invited the king and Haman to join her and dine.
At the end of the first meal she invited them back,
To discuss her real plan with grace and tact.
She asked the king if he would see her dead.
She told him about Haman and he was put to death instead.
Now Haman's deed had to be undone,
If the ultimate war was ever to be won.
So the king issued a decree and sealed it with his ring,
And before too long the Jews could once again be happy and sing.

Esther

23

Job - Faithful At All Cost

Job was a wealthy man, but he was faithful and true.
He loved God, was upright, and shunned evil too.
He had a large amount of livestock, that brought him great wealth.
And a very large household, all in good health.
Then one day Satan happened to show his face,
He was looking for a victim to condemn the whole human race.
God said to Satan you may try as you might,
But Job my faithful servant is just and right.
Satan figured Job would curse his God,
If he made a road that was difficult to trod.
So he took away Job's cattle first,
Hoping that Job, his God would have cursed.
Then Satan destroyed Job's sheep, camels and children.
He knew that Job would have to curse God then.
Job was devastated, but handled it well.
He fell on his knees, and decided to God, his troubles he would tell.
Satan figured if it was not enough to take Job's wealth,
Perhaps he would curse God if he took his health.
So he covered Job with boils from his feet to his head.
Job was tormented, but praised the Lord that he wasn't dead.

True Job cursed the day he was born,
But the name of the Lord he did not scorn.
Job's friends were not much help at all,
Trying to convince him that somewhere
he'd sinned and managed to fall.
Job began to question, but not curse God.
Why was his path so difficult to trod.
God spoke to Job in a whirlwind filled with power,
For he heard Job's voice beginning to sour.
God questioned Job and began to say,
Were you there on creations day?
And are you indeed mature enough,
To explain to me why the forces of nature can be so tough?
Job admitted and said he was vile,
For he did not want to put God on trial.
The Lord told Job to dispense with his wrath,
And warned him to continue on the righteous path.
Job admitted that he had heard of God but never saw,
The power of His strength or the mercy of His law.
Job repented for placing demands on his God,
And the Lord above spared him from the wrath of his rod.
His comforters though, felt the wrath from above,
When God demanded from them an offering of love.
So they did as god had wanted done,
And Job's long battle was about to be won.
He prayed a prayer to God above,
To spare his friends and show them love.
That's when God restored Job's health,
Brought back his cattle, his family and doubled his wealth.

So if we are ever faithful and true,
God will bless both me and you.

Job

My Provider

The Lord is my provider.
He gives me all I need.
He lets me rest by quiet waters,
And gives me fruit from what once was seed.
I try to do the things that praise His
Name at any cost,
And He guides me through the darkness so I
never can get lost.
He takes the fear away from me,
And gives me light so I may see.
He lets me know that I'm never alone,
Though it seems the battles fought are on my own.
His blessings pour out over me.
And since I trust in Him, I will always be free.
All through my life, He'll stand by my side,
Holding the door to heaven open wide.

Psalms 23:1-6

The Call Of Wisdom

The voice of wisdom can be heard from afar,
Whether walking in the rain or driving in the car.
Her voice calls aloud, and to listening ears,
She can calm all the storms, and ease all the fears.
The spirit of wisdom speaks simple words, and to those that heed,
She fulfils every wonder, desire or need.
But with those who do not listen, she becomes quite upset,
For if mocking they give, then mocking they will get.
Simple ones, they are called, those easily led astray,
Will make fun of wisdom until their dying day.
Then when destruction comes rushing into their life like a mighty storm,
They will call on her and seek her, but will not see her form.

Proverbs 1: 20-33

Joy And Wisdom

Eat your bread with joy and drink with a happy heart
For now you are indeed a part
Of God's glorious family above,
That's based on heavenly, not earthly, love.
Life as we mere humans know it is far too short and has much pain,
We must learn to enjoy the good, that we all, eventually attain.
Do not strive to obtain only worldly success,
For it will only make your life a mess.
Remember the little things that make you smile.
Reflect on them, and give God thanks for a while.
For we do not know when God will decide,
To have us embark on that glorious ride.
The ride to heaven's magnificent gate,
Where only joy and happiness, for us, await.
In all this, have the wisdom to know what is right.
For this is the best way to have favor in God's precious sight.

Ecclesiastes Chapters 8 and 9.

Solomon's Song for Us

We as believers can call ourselves the bride of Christ our King.
As lowly, people His love and forgiveness, is more desirable then anything.
We are defiled through the sin of Adam but made acceptable by
God's Holy Grace.
He loves us though we are not worthy to look upon His holy face.
We desire Him as our Shepherd and to keep us from harm.
With Him as our head, we need have no alarm.
We as believers are fair in the sight of Christ our Lord
For He gives us something stronger then any sword.
We by ourselves are puffed up but weak,
However, in Christ we will find the strength we seek.
We are a dove with Christ as our rock
He shields us and protects us when others mock.
He calls us and asks us to freely speak
However, prayerful communion is what He does seek.
Troubles comes fast and it is hard to see,
The face of Christ that sets us free.
The sin of the world is like a wilderness to the just
However, Christ will lead us out and take us home to a place of safety
and of trust.

Realizing we are imperfect and impure,
We strive to be nourished by the gospel, knowing that it is the only cure.

Song of Solomon Chapters 1-4

Are We Israel

God's own children stood up against Him in sin,
Thinking that they had what it takes to win.
He speaks of Jerusalem as Sodom and Gomorrah,
backslidden and away from God
As we speak of cities in our own country as such, destroying fertile sod.
Attitude is more important then action in the eyes of the Lord.
Willingness in the heart means more then
just slaying offerings with the sword.
The curse of the church has always been
As long as you contribute it's all right to sin.
God does not hear the prayers of those who continue to do wrong.
He is only interested in the heartfelt song
A full pardon by grace not works is available to all,
If you do not accept this, surely you will fall.
We are guilty of worshiping the works of man ahead of the creator
We will be brought to our knees sooner or later.
Children will assert themselves against their parents
And beautiful smells will be replaced by horrid scents.

Isaiah 1-2

God's Prophet

Even before the birth of this mortal man
God in His wisdom knew that He would tell Judah of His plan.
Jeremiah was hesitant at first,
He was scared and nervous without the spirit filled thirst.
But God from His heavenly throne
Said this is what I expect from you, so do not moan.
God put a finger on Jeremiah's mouth and wanted him to hear
The words he spoke were God's words and he had nothing to fear.
The Lord gave Jeremiah a vision, which was clear as day,
Of the destruction of Judah if they did not change their evil way.
He warned these people, through Jeremiah,
that what they were doing was wrong.
However, they continued to sing their wicked song,
Scorning God in heaven above,
Worshiping idols, and saying that lust was love.
Jeremiah did not want to be the bearer of bad news,
But it seemed he had an unusually long fuse.
He gave them fair warning as God gives to all
They chose to ignore it, and so came their fall.

It is wise to listen to warnings from God,
For there will not be surprises on the road you trod.

Jeremiah 1-3

The Silent City

Jeremiah looked down over the once thriving city
Now desolate and without pity
Jerusalem was destroyed for its multitude of sins
Moreover, it could happen to our cities, if the devil wins.
Jeremiah is saddened by this sight
Although he knew, what was done was right.
They had been warned but did not heed,
For the law of the Lord, they felt there was no need.
Jeremiah had seen the wrath of God's judgement
That is the reason for his lament.
Yet in the midst of total despair
He realized that God really did care.
He changed his thoughts from those of 'me'
To thoughts of 'Thee'
The desolation was a testimony of God's faithfulness.
He did exactly what He said He would do in all of His holiness.
Faithful to the just and the unjust
The Lord does not get pleasure from chastisement but,
discipline His children He must.

This book never needed to be written had His people listened to His Word
They could not say that it was not heard.
They were warned, as we are, repeatedly
Until God finally showed His faithfulness unmercifully

Lamentations

A Sinking Ship

We are all on board a sinking ship.
Making lots of money and trying to be hip.
Some Christians shout Glory to God on high
Rich on the outside but inside wanting to cry
The Global economy is doing quite well,
However, some Christians are spiritually broke and going to HELL.
Financial security is their god alone.
They get prideful, and to the devil's temptations, they are prone.
As the king of Tyre we adorn ourselves with all that is nice
But, leaving God out of the picture comes with a high price.
All the wealth and riches that we have obtained,
By God alone was preordained.
The warnings are many and we should listen and heed,
For there will come a time when we are in the greatest of need.
The devil wants us to take God out of our sight.
For then, he can take us without even a fight.
Continually we should be on our knees,
Praising God and praying that He hears our pleas.
He offers us a lifeboat that is ours to get in.
He'll put a cover over us but we have to stay away from prideful sin.
We are not better then God above,
He is the only one that really knows love.
We have to give ourselves completely to Him that we adore,
Only then can we escape the ship and make it safely to the shore.

Ezekiel 28

Daniel In the Lion's Den

Daniel was a mighty man, and in a position of power,
But his enemies sought to plan his demise right to the very hour.
They could find no wrong within this man
So they had to use deceit to fulfill their plan.
They built a statue in honor of the king,
And said for thirty days all would worship this thing.
The king saw no harm and figured some respect might be won,
So he signed the decree, which could not be undone.
Daniel was faithful to God above,
And continued to pray for His mercy and love.
So his enemies assembled in front of his house,
Ready to play a game of cat and mouse.
They went back to the king and reminded him of his decree,
And pointed out that Daniel was breaking the law, it was plain to see.
The king, upset with himself, for not thinking ahead,
Sent Daniel to the lions, actually hoping he would not wind up dead.
The king got no sleep, and fasted through the night.
He went to the lion's den at the dawn's first light.
The king was shocked to see Daniel alive.
For God sent an angel to help him survive.
When the king learned the plan of these evil men
He sent them and their families to the lion's den.
The lions killed them all you see,
And soon the king signed another decree.
That all would worship the living God, who truly saves,
His faithful followers from early graves.

Daniel Chapter 6

Hosea Takes a Prostitute for His Bride

Hosea was instructed by God to take a prostitute as his wife.
By doing this he ultimately saved her life.
She bore a son who was named Jezreel.
This prophetic name meant "cast-away", a name of shame in Israel.
It was a warning from God that He wanted His people to heed.
They would be cast from His kingdom and never be freed.
Yet another was born to Hosea and his wife,
And another sign of the Jew's ill-fated life.
Loruhamah was this child's name
And the meaning was yet another sign that God was tired of this game.
Her name meant, "not pitied" and this was sad
God had warned them but now he was mad.
Yet another baby was born to this household
And was named Loammi as God had foretold.
"Not My People" was the meaning of the third child's name.
Hopefully now God's people would become more tame.
But still one more thing had to be done.
Gomer, Hosea's wife, had to leave him to have some fun.
She finally wound up being sold as a slave.
But there was one last thing Hosea could do in order for her life to save.
He bought her back from the auctioneer
And once again vowed she had nothing to fear.
From that day forward she was faithful and true,
And her dedication could be matched by few.

Hosea Chapter 1

Joel, Prophet for Today

The 'Day of the Lord is at hand'
Not just a slogan, but a warning to an
ungodly land.
Joel saw then, what people were made of.
And most certainly it was not compassion
and love.
Joel warned God's people to sound the
alarm.
This was to warn everyone of the
impending harm.
Once again God had to take His mighty hand,
To cleanse and purify a defiled land.
We as people today do not differ much.
We choose to ignore God's gentle touch.
We participate in unclean things,
And do not hear the alarm when it rings.

Change your ways so you will indeed hear,
And know that the Day of the Lord is once
again near.

Joel 1:15 – 3:21

The Shepard With A Message

Amos was a sheepherder, and at his job he did quite well,
But God had a message for the 12 tribes that no one else could tell.
So He gave this job to Amos to do,
Because Amos loved the Lord and to His Word was true.
God looks to the motives, as well as the action.
Professed Christians are dealt with more harshly,
when they fall prey to sin's attraction.
The power of the 12 tribes was unrighteous when obtained,
And therefore their ultimate destruction was preordained.
Israel is then called on to truly seek the Lord,
And take comfort in knowing the mercy of His Word.
For the same God that can cast mighty judgments on mankind
Can give redemption and forgiveness to break Satan's bind.
Evil Israel had many times passed by the judgments of God's dread.
Now it is through the path of judgment that they must tread.
They are complacent in their relationship with God above.
Their morals are based on pride and self-love.
These people were too much at ease
And figured they could get away with as much as they please.
The rich and powerful were most guilty of this,
Because it was nothing more then common work that they did miss.
But despite all the turmoil and all that is bad
Christ's coming is predicted, and in that day, all will be glad

Amos

Prophet of Despair, Prophet of Repair

Obadiah was a messenger sent to give Edom a word from God above,
They were basing their security on things of earthly love.
A mighty Lord would bring them to their knees,
Their enemies would enter their city and take as much as they please.
Their barbarous treatment of Gods chosen people, the Jews,
Was the spark that lit their fuse
And set it burning until their final demise
As their city was being decimated right before their eyes.

And to the Jews came a promise of restoration,
That they might once again be a prosperous nation.
Much of this prophecy has been fulfilled
When the Jews returned to Israel without being killed.
The rest will occur when Christ makes his final return
And His eyes like a mighty fire will burn.

Obadiah

Jonah, Reluctant Prophet

Jonah was a prophet with a job to do
He was to go to Nineveh, and tell them that God was through.
Unless they changed their wicked way,
It would very soon be their judgment day.
But Jonah did not want to do this deed, and was full of dread,
So he had thought from God he had fled.
He jumped on a boat to Tarshish across the sea,
Where he figured he could finally be free.
But God sent a storm and tossed the boat,
It could barely even stay afloat.
The shipmasters were scared and wanted the passengers to pray,
And ask their own God for mercy this day.
They approached Jonah while he was asleep.
Was the storm punishment for a commandment he did not keep?
When questioned as to why,
Jonah did not attempt to lie.
He knew he was responsible for this terrible deed,
And had to do something so the others could be freed.
Reluctantly the mariners threw Jonah over the side,
But he was swallowed by the fish, and lived though he should have died.
After three days of prayer in the belly of the fish,
To be back in God's favor was Jonah's only wish.
So God showed mercy upon Jonah's soul
And the fish spit him out on dry land, fully whole.
But Jonah still had to complete the task
And do what at first God did ask.
This he did and the city repented.
God spared them and Jonah vented.
He felt he should have been spared God's wrath,
Even though he strayed from the righteous path.
Now he asked God to die because he was sad
This is clearly sinful and bad.
We should rejoice when God spares a sister or a brother
For the joy of a repented sinner is like no other

Jonah

39

Micah, It's all in a Name

A country preacher, who spoke to common man.
Micah tried to warn people of the Lord's holy plan.
'Who is like God' was what his name meant,
And to find a godly man, was why he was sent.
God would judge Judah for their evil way
Because they knew better but refused to obey.
Fierce armies would wreak havoc across the land.
This was totally done by God's own hand.
For Micah sought godliness from the delegated leaders of these towns.
What he found, instead of honesty was corruption,
and instead of smiles, frowns.
Destruction would be spread far and wide,
Throughout the entire countryside.
But fear not persecuted one
For God has a plan to send His Son.
We are given the exact location of Jesus birth,
And it is quite likely the lowliest place on earth.
But this is unimportant to God above
For all He was concerned with was hope and love.
We cannot use religion as a way back into God's good grace.
We must always live in love and mercy, if we are not to tremble
When we see God's face.

Micah

Nineveh's Destruction

Nineveh had their chance when Jonah spoke to them 100 years before
However, they decided being true to God was too much of a chore.
So once again God sent a messenger, this is true
Nahum told them their party was through.
No turning back no turning away
Soon God would bring them to their knees to show them the way.
Their destruction was laid out plain and clear
They were a city that trembled in fear
When God says He's against you there is trouble indeed
Like a gardener in a vegetable patch pulling the weed
This place needed to be cleaned up so God took a stand
And brought them to justice with his mighty hand
Assyria also would come under God's wrath
Because they walked down the evil path
The light they walked in while serving God
Would have protected them from anyone's rod
But because they sinned against the light
They felt the sting of God's pure might

Nahum

41

Comfort In Troubled Times

Despair not oh children of God
He knows the road you walk is not easily trod.
Remember as you go through life's pains,
That God in heaven above reigns.
Let our thoughts and actions be not like wolves of the night.
They are foreboding shadows that fill us with fright.
When filled with anger and fear
We tend to forget that God is here.
Walking beside us each step of the way
Ready to slay the wolves before the break of day.
But in order for Him to perform that wondrous task,
We must fall on our knees and humbly ask.
Then and only then will God step in,
Waging the war that only He can win.
We must admit that the enemy is too much for us alone
For without God's intervention we will never kneel before His throne.

Habakkuk

All Or Nothing

Total and utter destruction is the promise here.
Let all who are double minded, tremble in fear.
You cannot live for heaven's riches and also earthly desire.
If you do you will surely be consumed by the fire.
If you give Satan half you give him all.
If you give God half you give Him nothing at all.
The day of the Lord is truly at hand,
And He alone will judge a sin filled land.
Secure people are the one's to be reckoned with,
For they live a life that is based on myth,
That God will neither do good or bad
Life based on this philosophy is truly sad.
They miss the promises of God's reward
And do not fear the consequences of His sword.
Realize this and repent right now
Do not be a weed under the Master's plow.

Zephaniah

Not Yet?

If we linger too long time may slip away
Do God's work now, before the judgment day
Never say, "I'll do it, but just not yet"
For with all of life's issues you may just forget
And do His work with all purity in your heart
For if sin is on your mind you shouldn't even start
These sinful people neglected building God's holy place
Figuring they could obtain more by serving the human race
They were wrong and the price they paid was high
Famine plagued them and their land was barren and dry
The people returned to God and did as they should
And began to rebuild the temple as best as they could
While not completed, at least their heart was right
And through God's mercy they were given sight
Now people began to live for God and His mercy flowed out
The famine cleared up and so did the drought

Haggai

The Revelation Of The Old Testament

God sent Zechariah visions of things to come,
And they all add up to a dreadful sum.
For the sinner that does not have God in their life,
Will walk a road filled with constant strife.
The flying scrolls in chapter five
Show only God's people will survive
Since all have all sinned and fallen short of the law
The only way to save us is through what Zechariah later saw
The coming Messiah, who will put an end to all war,
And whom on bended knee all men will adore
Yes Zechariah was truly a visionary man
God showed him His entire plan
If this book is studied very closely
A map through the entire New Testament you will see.
Follow it and let it be your guide
And God, through His son will always be by your side

Zechariah

Eternal Forgiveness

God's love for his people is shown in this book,
But also His expectations, if we take a closer look.
Clergy especially, have a lot on their plate,
But if they do not follow through they will face a horrible fate
God curses for disobedience each and every day
As He blesses for obedience when you follow His way
God is faithful and always true
And though one slips He'll return to you.
But repent you must,
In order to regain His trust.
By following basic rules like tithing ten percent
Shows that you indeed do want to repent

Malachi

New Testament

GRACE

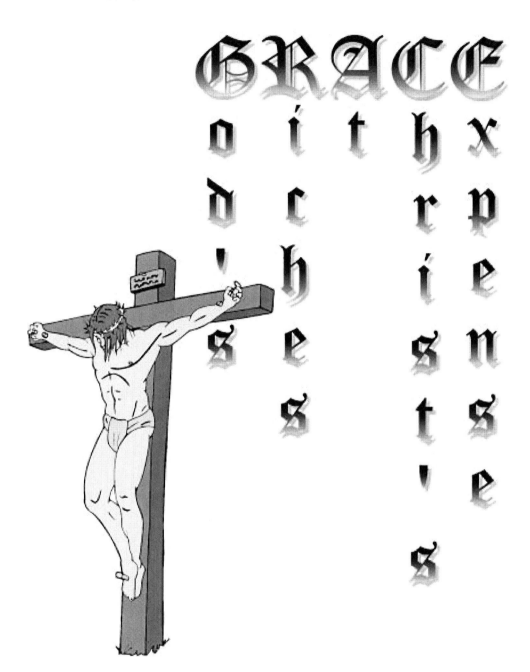

God's riches at Christ's expenses

The Birth Of Our King

God sent an angel to talk to Mary,
And informed her that the Savior of the world she would carry.
There would be no fanfare for the birth of this king,
In fact, most of the world would not even know of this glorious thing.
Joseph was upset when he learned of her state,
They were going to be married, but he considered breaking the date.
As he slept one night, an angel appeared,
And explained to him that things were not as he feared.
He should go on with his plans and take Mary for his bride,
Moreover, they would raise a King standing side by side.
Now there were wise men three,
Who were anxious to see
The birth of their Savior and King.
However, Herod had ideas of his own,
And felt he was the only one entitled to sit on the throne.
So he called the wise men before him,
And asked them to come back and say,
The exact location where Jesus did lay.
They agreed and went on, being led by the star's bright light,
To the spot in Bethlehem, that was the chosen site.
And when they arrived they were filled with joy,
At the precious sight of the new born baby boy.
They gave him gifts and sang a song,
But then they had to hurry along.
They were told by the angels that appeared in a dream,
To go right home and not fall for Herod's scheme.

Matthew 1:18 – 2:12

An Angry Jesus

Jesus rode into town not as a conqueror
but as a humble servant of God above.
His whole teaching was one based on love.
However, on this day he was angry and hurt,
As the people threw their garments down on the dirt.
They welcomed him into their city as a king.
Some people did not like the teaching he would bring.
As He neared the temple Jesus was hungry and saw a tree.
Hoping for a fig he drew near it happily.
When no fruit on the tree was there to be found,
Jesus cursed it and said it would whither to the ground.
Jesus still believed the temple was a Holy place.
But people were buying and selling and making it a disgrace.
Jesus was quite upset with all of this stuff,
And decided finally that enough was enough.
Roman money was no good here,
So the money had to be changed and the price was dear.
He told them to stop what they were doing,
For it did not make God the father happy.
The temple was supposed to be a house of prayer for all to see.
People were supposed to be able to worship for free.
The priests were all trying to get Jesus out of the way,
But it would be hard because of the
followers around Him both night and day.
They passed the tree again and it was withering and dying.
It dawned on Peter that Jesus had not been lying.
Jesus taught them about faith in God above. HE does not deceive.
For you can move a mountain if only you believe.

Mark 11:1-23

Prayer

Teach us to pray, oh Lord
Help us to better understand your word.
We know you are a friend so true,
And that we can always count on you.
As we stand at the door to your heavenly realm,
Your awesome majesty can overwhelm.
We must always remember that you are our friend,
And that the bread of heaven you will gladly send.
We can not possibly give this on our own,
It must come exclusively from your heavenly throne.
Hear us knocking, though it is late at night.
For only you can give us the heavenly light,
To give unto a dying world,
So they can see your heavenly banner unfurled.
Allow us to seek your heavenly face
And bask in the glory of your grace.
Answer us oh Lord when we ask for heavenly bread,
So a dying world can be fully fed.

Luke 11:1-10

Dead, No, He Lives

The cross is not to be viewed as a sign of pain,
But for the Christian it is a sign of gain.
Our Lord gave His all for us upon that tree,
As He conquered sin and death, and won the victory.
Two sinners on either side, who deserved to die,
But still, with him to heaven they would fly.
Saved by grace you too can be.
Christ paid your debt and set you free.
You can now stand before God above,
And say Your Son died for me to show his great love.
But that's not the end of the story, for there is more to tell.
Jesus descended to the very depths of hell.
He took the keys of death from Satan's hand,
And proclaimed life eternal for a sin filled land.
All you need to do is confess him as your Savior and Lord,
And your name in the book of life will be eternally stored.
But there is still more of the story that needs to be said,
For after three days, Christ our Lord and Savior, was no longer dead.
That's right folks He awoke from His slumber and sleep,
A silent vigil over lost souls to keep.
Showing us His mighty GLORY in every way,
When we as the body of Christ begin to pray

John 19:16 – 20:16

Do You Understand When They Speak

Watch the flame
As they praise His name
Filled with the Spirit,
Can you hear it?
The time of revival is here.
And though some are scared
There is really nothing to fear.
His name is Holy,
And this feat is from Him solely.
All who hear can understand
That this has all been previously planned.
The work of God, through His son,
Has got the devil on the run.
The church is rising from it's grave
And going out to the people that need to be saved.
The name of the Son is on every voice
So let all who hear shout and rejoice.
For the book of Acts has not been completed,
Nor shall it be until the devil is defeated.

Acts 2:1 - 14

If God Be For Us

We as Christians are among the few
Who can suffer all consequences and know what to do
The answer is really quite simple and plain
Just get on our knees and ask God to remove the pain
The people of old thought Noah was quite insane.
That was before it started to rain
God was for Noah, so it mattered not,
That know one else could see the plot.
Daniel as he stood in the lion's den
Knew God was for him even then
All the evil in the world today
Can do you no real harm if you follow the way
Christ, as He was nailed upon the cross
Knew this was a gain and not a loss
God, His Father, was for him this was true
Now let him for all eternity be for you
The one and only really true friend
That will stand beside you until the end.

Romans 8:31

A Writer's Love Chapter

Even though I can write beautiful words,
And my grammar and spelling are perfect
If I do not show love in my writing,
Then I am just taking up space on the page.
If my writing conveyed the events of the future,
And could predict the outcome of conflicts,
If I did not love others then my writing would be worthless.
Even if all my books became bestsellers,
They would not be worth the paper used to print them if I had not love.
If I gave all my royalties to charity, and did my best to aid other writers;
If I were thrown in jail for works, that praised God but did not love others,
My sacrifices would have been in vain.
Love is patient and kind.
It is never jealous of other writers who make more money.
Love never boasts or brags if a poem is sold.
Love does not demand to be the greatest.
It is not irritated even when the page in the typewriter is blank.
Love holds no grudge against the editor that sends a piece back
With a rejection, notice attached.
It is not happy when a new writer does not get a chance,
However, is happy when they break into a tough market.
When you love someone, you stand by him or her at all cost.
You always believe they can accomplish anything.
You will offer encouraging words to editors, they submit work to.
Abilities we now have will fade quickly,
But love will go on forever.
Someday language, books, and inspiration will end.
Writers know so little, although their gift for words touch
The hearts and souls of so many.
When we are made perfect by God's love,
The gifts we now have will end.
When I was a child, my writing showed immaturity,
However now that I am a man,
My writing speaks as a man.
I have given up my childhood fantasies.
The same holds true for our understanding of God.
Now we gave into a stagnant pond,
However when we accept God into our hearts,
We will be able to see clearly.
Remember: Plot, characterization, and grammar are all important in writing,
But nothing is more important then love

1 Corinthians Chapter 13

Suffering Brings Us Closer To Christ

Though trials may torment us and toss us to and fro
Christ is always a lighthouse showing us how to go.
The more pain invoked upon our mortal soul
Is more cement to make us whole
Look at suffering as a teaching tool
And pain as the final test in school.
The emptier our lives appear to be
Is when Christ steps in to set us free
When things are going good and all is well
We have no testimony that we can tell
Things must go wrong for many of us to hit our knees
And then be able to tell how Christ truly frees.
Think about this the next time things are going bad,
Did you tell anyone of the good times you had

Or is it only when you've hit your low
That you can tell someone that Christ is the answer
And way to go

2 Corinthians

Christ Sets You Free

Open your hearts and you will see,
That Christ alone can set you free,
From the curse of the law that no one could live by,
No matter how hard they try.
All of us are guilty under the law
God knew this and was disturbed by what He saw.
That's why He sent His only Son,
Who took on our sentence, fought death and the devil, and won!

So you see, there's no need to feel guilty when we slip and fall,
'Cause Jesus Christ took it all,
As He hung on the cross that fateful day
Showing us all that only HE is the way
As believers we become children of God above
Released from the bondage of the law by His unconditional love

We must realize that this is not a license to sin,
But a battle of guilt that need not be fought to win.
As an earthly father would,
Our heavenly Father quickly forgets the bad and remembers the good.

Galatians Chapter 3

Prepare For The Battle

Any soldier going into battle must know,
The proper equipment needed to counter the enemy's blow.
As Christians, we fight a far deadlier being
Then any human we can remember seeing.
We require special protection from the devil himself,
For he can take away a lot more then our health.
We must at all times wear the full armor of God above,
For it will protect us and surround us with love.
We must protect our loins with the truth of God and His son,
For this is a start at the war being won.
We must protect our heart with the breastplate of righteousness.
Our shoes should be those that walk in peacefulness.
For a shield, we should use our faith alone,
For it can deflect any opposition's stone.
To protect our head from the evil all around,
We must wear the helmet of salvation as we walk the battleground.
Finally, for offence we need to hold, the sword of the spirit,
Which is the Word of God, and that is stronger then the enemy is bold.

Satan does not want to deal with these things from above,
He cannot handle peacefulness, joy, and love

Ephesians 6:1-17

Humility

Conversation is not just talk,
But the lifestyle we lead and the walk we walk.
The gospel itself is simple and plain.
We must not intellectualize it with our brain.
Our lifestyle, dress, behavior and speech
Must reflect the gospel we try to preach.
Let us win others to Christ with a gentle hand
And not scare them off with an overzealous band
Praise music is fine; do not get me wrong
But there are times when a raucous beat does not belong.
Let humility and Godliness be our guide
As we try to win someone over to the Gospel side.
We as Christians need to differ from other people around
We must have our feet planted firmly upon the solid ground.
Let us pray for a Christ like attitude in adversity
Let us temper our minds and gain humility

Philippians

All Kindred

All true Christians are brothers and sisters in Christ our Lord
Who shall always be revered and adored
Faith, hope and love being prominent in Christian life
Will aide with us all, in times of stress and strife
Setting our sights on our heavenly reward
Will help us keep in focus, Christ, who is constantly adored
We must strive to remember the difference between worldly, carnal,
And Christian love
Remembering that only the last comes from the Holy Spirit,
And God above
Even in trials that we face from day to day
We must always thank God for His GRACE along the way

Colossians

Are You Thankful

We have so much to thank God for,
The stars that shine in the sky, the waves that crash upon the shore,
But we take it all for granted, and don't give God His due.
My friend today I'm thankful, and I hope that you are too.

Are you thankful that our Savior died on the cross for you?
Are you thankful that He turned your skies to the clearest blue?
When you take time to look at a flower in awe,
Are you truly thankful for what you saw?

God above is a giving God,
Who turns the barren ground into rich and fertile sod,
All He asks is that we thank Him and give Him what He's due.
My friend today I'm thankful, and I hope that you are too.

I am thankful when I look in the sky,
And even thankful when I hear a baby cry.
For each little star in the sky above,
And more thankful then ever for God's great love.

So think about this, each time you are blue:
When you are thankful to God, no harm can come to you.

1 Thessalonians 5:16-19

Coming Again? YES But We Know Not When

Satan is cunning and smart
He will promote errors even in Scripture and try to
Deceive the Christian heart
Whatever human errors occur about Christ's second reign
When the time is right He WILL indeed come again
False doctrines toss us to and froe
Caught in a storm with no oar to row
Expect and live your life though, that the time is always near
Be ready always but don't let Satan instill in you, fear
People will grow away from their faith in the last days
Leaving an open door for the Anti-Christ in many ways
Many signs and wonders will readily appear
It is Satan's way to cause wonder and fear
Do not let yourself be deceived by these things
Or you will receive the keys to hell that the Anti-Christ brings

2 Thessalonians 2 : 1-12

Christian Duties

We must pray for all people not just those close to us
No need to condemn, criticize or fuss
Our duty as Christians is plain to see
There are two things we need to be.
Godly, through the right worshipping of God above
And honest in showing good conduct
towards all people whom God does love
The two must go together hand in hand.
Only then will we have a Godly land
We are not confined to one particular house of prayer
As believers we are supposed to pray everywhere
Be it in the comfort of our own home,
With many people or all alone
Pastors must not have skeletons of their past life
For it will cause discord and strife
They should seek to help one another all the time
For being called by God to the ministry is truly sublime
God will carry them through the roads
And in the end will help to lighten their load

1 Timothy Chapters 2 and 3

Christian Learning

Person of doubt who's soul is so dear,
God has not given us the spirit of fear.
He has given us the spirit of courage,
There is no need to be discouraged.
Any affliction that may come down the line
We will deal with and the outcome will be just fine

We must not only teach children ABC's
But more importantly what the bible decrees
As it has an answer for every situation
And provides us all with true revelation
In these our very last days
We must be careful about our ways

We must never grow bored with the gospel of the Lord
For He must always be worshipped and adored
If we stand fast through stress and strife
We may very well lose our earthly life
But that is not the important thing here
For with our faith in Christ we have nothing to fear.

2 Timothy

Titus and the Three Ls

Leave your life of old, far behind.
Live the new life that you will find
Look to Christ for hope and blessing
Change your ways after confessing.
Are you holy at home as well as in the pew?
How you are out of church tells a lot about you.
Live a life that makes others want what you've got
Show people you are not doomed to be part of Satan's lot.
Though we are not saved by our good works alone,
We should want to do good before we stand at the throne.
The blueprint for church membership can be found in this book,
All you have to do is take a look.
It speaks to men, women, employees, and youth
And what was true then, is still today the truth.

Titus

Forgiveness

When wronged, we are to forgive.
The reason for this is so we can live,
A life that's pure and clean
So no blemish on us can be seen
Onesimus was wrong; there was no denying his deed
But he found Christ, repented, and was truly freed.
This short book serves as an object lesson for us all
To take the same position as the apostle Paul
Good thing for us Jesus did just that thing
For now we are able to praise His name and sing
For he heard my plea
Took my sins and set me free

Philemon

FAITH

By faith we can not only do, but also accept all things.
Trials on earth are minor compared to flying away on heavenly wings.

Those who trusted in the prophets of old,
Should place their trust in Jesus so bold.
For even angels bow to Him and obey.
He is more powerful then mere words can say.
Do not neglect to listen to Christ the Son,
He is above everything and everyone.

Moses was a servant but Jesus is the master
It is only He who can lead us to the greener pasture.
Do not harden your heart and resist God's lead,
Because only He can fulfill every need.
Never think you've done all that you can do,
Because no matter how much is completed, God is not done with you.

A high priest is appointed to offer sacrifices for sin
But placing your faith in a priest, you will not win.
Christ is always available to answer your call.
With your faith in Him you cannot fall.

Hebrews Chapters 1-5

The Sharp Sword Of The Tongue

Friends on earth please be aware,
Your words can cause pain, as well as speak in prayer.
Of all the sins, we can seem to control,
Our speech is the toughest as a whole.
If the words of God are upon your lips,
You can avoid potentially dangerous slips.
For the tongue it seems can be the spark,
That starts the fires of hell to burn in the dark.
Always build up and never tear down,
So your mouth can wear a smile instead of a frown.
We can tame animals with no problem at all,
However, taming our tongues requires that we listen to God's divine call.

One never finds an orange on an apple tree.
Likewise, a Christian can not have a vulgar mouth and expect to be free.
Remember we need to build people up, whatever the cost.
For if we do not, our souls shall be eternally lost.
Do not let your speech cause you to stray.
Glorify God, speak well of your brother, and be happy today.

James Chapter 3

Strength Through Suffering

Rejoice indeed, for the temptations you now face are but a season.
Be assured that God above put them before you for a reason.
For when gold is tempered by fire it becomes more precious then before,
As you will gain strength with each victory, and love God even more.
Protect your mind and be vigilant in your faith of God above.
Know that He will not falter in His love.
Be as a child and always obey, whatever God tells you, in whatever way.
Do not base your life on the past you lived, for that was then, another day.
Be holy in all manners of living and speech.
For your actions may be what God is using to teach.
Submit yourself to every law of man
For it's up to you to do all you can.
Remember beloved that the flesh is like grass
And all too quickly it will come to pass
That the grass will die, only to be reborn in the next season.
This is God's plan for believers alone,
To die on earth and live again in heaven to sit by His throne.

1 Peter 1:6-24

The Lord Shall Return

Be aware, though the scoffers may doubt,
That the day of the Lord is coming about.
Let the words of the bible put to rest all your fears.
A day with the Lord is as a thousand years.
The Lord wants no ear to not have heard,
Of the beauty and counsel of His precious word.
The Lord is patient and will continue to wait,
Until all have been told of the beauty beyond heaven's gate.
To hasten the return of our savior and Lord,
We must put on the armor and pick up the sword.
We must tell all the world of the coming day,
When the earth as we know it shall pass away.
Always be ready for the time is at hand,
When all believers will be taken to the promised land.
There will be no announcement to let you know.
Only the faithful will be invited to go.

2 Peter Chapter 3

Walking In The Light

God is light, and will guide you with a beacon from above.
But you must walk in the light to feel His mercy and love.
We can not simply say we walk in the light,
And stray into darkness when day turns to night.
If we claim to be without a single sin,
Then surely we lie and will be stained within.
But if we confess and are sorry indeed,
Jesus the Son will speak to God the Father, and we will be freed.
We can not claim to know God, and not follow His commands.
To walk as Jesus did is what the bible commands.
We can not claim to live in the light and hate our brother.
For to walk in the light, you can hate no other.
Father, say to your son, "If the word of God lives in you,
Then you can defeat the evil one."
Do not love the world here below,
For the tempest of darkness will toss you to and fro.
No matter what you obtain it will someday be in the past,
But the man who does God's will, shall have a life that forever will last.
If you see a man who is down and out in the city,
Give him some clothes and show him some pity.
For if this thing you always do,
Then the light of God's love will shine on you.

1 John 1:5 – 3:16

Beware Of The Deceivers

As the Father above declared
When your children walk in the truth, their joy by you will be shared.
There is within here, not a new command,
But one we should have heard from the start.
Love one another and walk in God's commands,
Follow His will with all your heart.
If you follow this command and walk in love,
God will allow His great mercy to shine down from above.
There are many in the world who do not believe.
Their only purpose is to tear down and deceive.
Do not lose all that you have worked for.
Your rewards in heaven will be all you imagined and even more.
Whoever runs ahead and teaches not of Jesus
Does not have God in their heart.
They are doomed to destruction, right from the start.
Do not let them enter your home,
For if you do, you share in their evil, and forever in misery you will roam.

2 John

Hospitality

Hospitality is an important part of our Christian walk,
People must know we speak the truth when we talk.
Always open your house to your fellow man,
It is part of God's glorious heavenly plan.
If you do this with joy in your heart,
Then God, to you, His blessings will impart.
Offer a pastor a bite to eat,
And indeed you accomplish a heavenly feat.
Your soul will be blessed beyond compare,
And you'll walk down the street without a care.
But if you are not gracious to one who preaches the Word,
Then your requests to God just may not be heard.
Do not imitate evil and say you are good.
Imitate purity and truth is what you should.
For as the Christians we profess to be,
People around us should plainly see,
That we live for God in all we do,
Praising His name and doing only what is true.

3 John

Reject False Teachers

To those who are called, be led not astray,
By the false teachers that are among us today.
You have been chosen by God and sanctified,
And you know that He in heaven should be glorified.
Be upright, loving and pure,
For the judgment of God shall be delivered against the unholy for sure.
Do not reject the authority from above,
Because our God is wrathful as well as full of love.

These false teachers care nothing for people, but lead them astray.
The only way to avoid them is if we pray.
They are like clouds in the sky that hold no rain.
They only cause darkness, suffering and pain.
They will flatter you to gain your trust,
Then try to fill you with lies and worldly lust.
Remember the words in the bible are true.
If it's not in there then it's not for you.

Jude

Revelation

We needn't face the coming tribulation at all,
If only on the name of Christ we call.
We can all be taken to heaven and not have to see,
The total devastation of land, water, animal and tree.
Confess now, every man woman and child,
The name of Jesus before things really get wild.
His children will be spared,
Because for them He really cared.
All others though are in deep trouble,
For the deceiver will come and much of the earth will be turned to rubble.

But even if you are left behind,
Salvation and truth you'll still be able to find.
As long as no matter, the times how dark,
You never ever take the mark.
For if you do, your eternal life is done,
And you'll never be able to live with the Son.

This poem is too short for all that must be said,
So I plead with you, the book of Revelation must be entirely read.
Do it now before it's too late,
Because how you view it's outcome will determine your eternal fate.

Revelation

Index Of Scriptural References Used In This Book

You Don't Need to die eternally

Jesus said,
"I AM THE DOOR, IF ANYONE ENTERS BY ME,
HE WILL BE SAVED..." John 10:9.
The Bible says:
"FOR WHOSOEVER SHALL CALL UPON THE NAME OF THE LORD
SHALL BE SAVED." Romans 10:13.

Prayer of Salvation

Lord I am a sinner, please help me I pray:
Just simply to make it through another day.
I want your son Jesus to enter my heart
To take over my soul and make me a part,
Of your Holy family once and for all
So that I may never ever again fall.
I know that Jesus died for my sin
And with Him in my heart I can do nothing but win.

Lightning Source UK Ltd.
Milton Keynes UK
UKOW010008280213

206893UK00002B/21/P